AF351674

This Book about Nothing

David Lawrence

Copyright© 2020 David Lawrence
ISBN: 978-93-88319-22-5

First Edition: 2020
Rs. 200/-

Cyberwit.net
HIG 45 Kaushambi Kunj, Kalindipuram
Allahabad - 211011 (U.P.) India
http://www.cyberwit.net
Tel: +(91) 9415091004 +(91) (532) 2552257
E-mail: info@cyberwit.net

No part of this book may be reproduced or transmitted in any form or by any means, electronic, mechanical, photocopying, or otherwise, without the express written consent of David Lawrence.

Printed at Repro India Limited.

Contents

The Voices are Death

Seeing My Neurologist

I went to see Dr. Charney this morning. He's at 1111 Park Avenue among the classy doctors, near some of my rich friends.

He is a neurologist. I took a bus. I became confused as to whether I was going uptown or downtown. My sense of direction was beaten out of me.

Why would I need a neurologist? Because I am seventy years old. Because I was hit in the head fifty thousand times when I was boxing. Because I was knocked out cold in both an amateur and a pro fight. Because I was knocked down in sparring and once forgot if I had boxed that day. My thoughts conflicted with each other and hurt the direction of clarity.

I had to wait in his reception room for an hour. It always goes like that. I once walked out. I get claustrophobic when I am trapped in someone else's discretion.

It was nice to see Dr. Charney in is private office. He has a good sense of humor for a Brainiac. We chatted about the movie they are doing on my life story. He said that the fact that I got upfront money shows that the producer is sincere.

On a previous MRI it showed I had some water on my brain. Not an ocean. Maybe a puddle. He had his nurse call in a prescription for me to dry up the water. He said there were no side effects.

He said the first time I use the drug it is a bit of a diuretic. I told him I'd try it on Sunday when I am not out and about. I am scared of pissing in public.

I made an appointment for a month away. I don't really know if there is anything wrong with me. Except forgetfulness, failed direction, confusion, losing people's names and not remembering I saw a movie the day before.

It's like my being bipolar and not knowing it. Every doctor says that I am. I just think I am nice. I melt into situations like ice. Will a psychiatric classification suffice? Will I win if I just roll out the dice? Will there be holes in my brain from the teeth of the mice biting into cheese?

Stay Awhile

Well, it's another day and I am not another person. I am the same old David that fills myself with essence like a balloon.

I pinch myself and discover that I have a hand. My forearm is black and blue. I love you and you and me.

Whatever I be I be because I am the essence of congealed superficiality. I am putty. I am my own buddy.

I dance on the head of a pin. I am an angel. I am carrying my afterlife on my shoulders like a father carrying his son.

Does it matter? Death is an irrelevancy undercut by its own resolution and the future doesn't matter when it is pounced by the upcoming past.

To be honest, I want to grab life by the throat and strangle the future out of it so that I stay awhile like the song says. "Stay awhile, what's your hurry?/Stay awhile 'cause I worry, oh/Any time that you're out of sight."

That was Dusty Springfield. She's dead. We're all dead or dying. I would miss my living if I could.

I worry when I am out of sight. I sometimes escape myself and can't find my face in a forest of contradictory thoughts. There are rabbits in the wood. I eat them and feel ashamed.

Blimp

Blimp tells me to buy him some Coconut Water. He is three hundred and fifty pounds and used to spar with Tyson.

"You got to be kidding. I haven't taught one student today. I got no money," I say.

Leon, the Bull, Taylor gives me two dollars for Blimp's water. The snack stand is only ten feet away. I don't know why Blimp needs me to get it.

I get the Water. I also get some potato chips. When I bring them back Blimp laughs, "See I got the white boy to run an errand."

Am I the white boy? I guess I am. But I am more than that. I am not a color or the absence of color.

I am a Ph.D., a pro boxer, a man who has been married forty-five years, an author, a father, a person on the fringe of the mentally ill, a former CEO, an ex con and a used-to-be model.

I am also creeping closer to death. I am seventy years old. I used to be chauffeured in my Rolls Royce. I am preparing the drapes for my trip in my hearse.

Wow, I'm Old

I am a body. I am a soul. I am an am. I am bacon and ham. I am a Jew. What will I do when I become a religion and they throw rice after me like Christ?

I am love. I am a muscle. I give myself a tussle when I stare at a woman's bustle. I don't. I am not. I am the hardening of snot in my nose

I am a rose. I grows. I am the garden that was in Montauk for thirty years. I don't die because life is a breeze.

I freeze when my blood grows cold. I am really old. I am seventy although I look like I am twelve. I flip a hoola hoop around my hips even though I don't have one. I am my father's son. I am the sun.

I am God's fury. I am wary of greatness. I am afraid I will grow too large and charge down a river like a barge.

There are circus animals on my deck. What the heck. I am what I am and am what I am not. Life is such and a lot.

I am glad that I took this venture. When people look at me they go blind. They can't stand that they can't see what I am all about.

A Realistic Alternative

I have led a life on a mountain path. I was riding a donkey. I was an ass. I was tomorrow's story in yesterday's predilection.

Where am I going? How does the ledge slip away from me and how do I fall off the cliff when I am tied to this life by ropes?

Death is a realistic alternative to breathing through a feed bag. I don't really care if I die. I am the absence in ambition and the cold joy in a dance on a glacier.

I will draw a card to see how much longer I have to go. I pull an ace of spades. That is either death or life. I am gambling with my future.

There is something about having been here so long that makes time an aside and I step out of range.

Where am I going? Is life so dispensable or is death so possible. Have I been here or have I not?

Will I be brushed into a dustbin? Or will I gather up with the world with my broom and spill it into my pockets.

Outer Space

My spaceship has just landed and I realize that I am on earth. I don't really fit in here because I am not enmeshed in the doldrums of inefficient life.

I know who I am because I know who you are not.

I take off my space suit as I adjust to the atmosphere of hypocritical roses in fake vases that are less than they present.

I am David from Mars. Or maybe from the moon? Or maybe Venus? I am the surprise of another planet on the Tupperware in a dining room.

When you look at me I see through you and know that I am the surprise that became the quotidian.

I don't matter. I am dying in an avalanche of poems and can only find meaning in my notes in the margins.

The Voices are Death

I am creeping towards the casket in the hole in the ground. I am the hole in the wall listening to the other voices in an adjunct wall.

The voices are death. I don't really mind it because what was given is always taken and I will adjust to my fall.

It's not that I don't like life because I do enjoy it and pleasure myself with being here with a smile on my serious face.

I have seen blindness and the aura of rotting bones in the devil-may-care casket where I play cards with the mice.

You don't know me when I cease to exist and I will become the sadness of death in the mirage of happy days.

Whether I live or die is irrelevant. Actually, death always wins and I flex my muscles to show that I will put up a good fight even though it will end so quickly.

Death in the Kennels

I have died and gone to doggie heaven amongst the poodles and the gray haired schnauzers.

Not really. But heck I am seventy and expect to soon hear the barking of death in the kennels.

I don't care. I don't know where I will be going or where I won't wander into the ashes of my cremation.

What's the difference when difference no longer makes a difference and death is a blank slate?

I come and go and go on the underside of a marked deck of cards as I win what I don't deserve to win and pull a tuna out of the sea for good luck.

I have suddenly gone fishing. I will die at the bottom of the sea with all my forget-me-nots which I have forgot.

Give It Up

I'd like to die but still be alive. I want to watch over my death like a sleeping bag in the woods where the trees have absconded.

I'm ready to give it up. I'm not. I am as indecisive as a grape about to fall from the edge of a table.

Give it up. What? Why? Now or never. I don't know. I like it here but not so much and the thought of dying while I am still alive is unpleasant.

I am climbing in the mountains and I am cold. There are holes in my snowshoes. I begin to freeze and I feel warm.

The coziness of death is a fabulous thing. It is disappearance into a crevice while I forget where I was climbing.

I know my absence for my presence and I can't seem to distinguish between corporal and a cloud.

This Book and Some People

This Book

I am writing this book about nothing. It doesn't exist. It is the lack of air in a vacuum.

There are covers on each side of the pagination. They keep out the digressions and imprint the lice.

I am what I am which is not who you are and you drift away on your only little canoe to disappearing islands.

You can't have my book. I don't even want you to read it. It is mine. It is time spread out into the choice of meaning.

I'd like to write on forever about nothing so that nothing becomes something bouncing against strangers' elbows.

I am what I don't say and I say what I don't under the broken lightbulb where truth is a beacon unto its glass on the table.

Lunch

I go out for lunch from Gleason's Gym to Forager's where I get my sushi in a small, flat, plastic container.

I usually get "Super Alaska." I don't know what's in it. I don't believe in intellectual dissection. Whatever it is it is and I am in love with it regardless.

Walking out I trip on my face. Actually, my face is braced by my hands which tingle-hurt.

I think of calling my wife, Lauren, and telling her I'm hurt. It's really nothing but I want some of her sympathy stirred up in a bowl like bouillabaisse.

I want to drink her affection and suck her up in a straw. She is like the sushi. I don't know what's in her but it all tastes good.

They say that the first sign of getting old is tripping and that it sometimes results in death from a broken bone or hip.

I don't want to worry Lauren that I am dying. I want to be taken away when she's not looking and I hope at that point she has Alzheimer's so that she doesn't have to be aware that I am gone.

The Wall

I am me and I be whatever I be because I am the wall that has disappeared into Mexico.

I am separated from closeness by the largeness of my borders and whatever I can't find is found in terrific isolation.

To be myself is to run from championship into a lake of intimacy where the water gathers me into its pail.

I have seen you in foreigners' faces but everything is foreign to me because I am the citizenship of gathered wool.

I speak one language because why should I trip along in broken Spanish or fractured French.

When I kiss you I am kissing myself because the deeper I get beneath my persona the more habitable I am in self-union.

I am the end of the leash where a dog lifts his leg and pisses on his rubber booties in the snow in a neat fashion.

I know myself because I don't want to know another where another is an intrusion into my seemly separation.

I Don't Care

I have died and gone to doggie heaven amongst the poodles and the gray haired schnauzers.

Not really. But heck I am seventy and expect to soon hear the barking of death in the kennels.

I don't care. I don't know where I will be going or where I will wander into the ashes of my cremation.

What's the difference when difference no longer makes a difference and death is a blank slate?

I come and go and go on the underside of a marked deck of cards as I win what I don't deserve to win and pull a tuna out of the sea for good luck.

I have suddenly gone fishing. I will die at the bottom of the sea with all my forget-me-nots which I have forgotten.

Run from the Runs

I have a stomach ache. I am dying. I am shot full of diarrhea. I disgust myself like a person who doesn't like the breakdown of his own biology.

It's tough to be a person. I'd rather be a goat. I'd be able to protect myself with my horns and get laid a lot in the shadow of a fence.

I take an Imodium. It always works on my shit. I slowly start to settle into the respite of normality and the calm of not knowing I am sick.

I am not sick. It's just a passing wave like pollution on the shore.

I like it when I am feeling good and don't follow the eruptions in my body. When I am healthy I don't know I exist because there is nothing to interfere with my quietude.

I want to disappear from my ailments. I want to rise into another life where peace is quiet and quiet is the lack of pain.

I don't want to be an upset stomach. I prefer to be my bipolar mind celebrating who I am and who I am not without the interference of my body.

Dudley

I have known Dudley since 1964 when I met him at the school bus stop in Great Neck Estates. He was the first kid I met in town. He was an anchor I threw into the Long Island Sound of isolation.

This morning we had our usual Sunday breakfast. I have known him off and on for fifty-four years. We have been inadvertently walking down the same suburban street forever.

There is something satisfying about taking a broom to your past in a dustbin of remembrances. It is stuffed and comfortable. It is a lounge chair on a wave.

We talk about death. It is not that far away. I have already settled with the gambling house and cashed my chips on the green felt table.

I know Dudley longer than my wife. No drama there. Just a friend that is comfortable like a space shoe. There is no divorce from a long term casual acquaintance. There is no divorce from a loving wife.

I was brought up in the sixties. Fidelity was considered a weakness and a sign that you can't enjoy variety in an orgy.

In 2018 the world has become multiracial. It's like it was when it was multi-orgasmic. Change is a terrible thing. It fails to find the consistency in tradition. The progressive world has not progressed. It has fallen into redundant clichés. It is so blindly sure of itself that it trips on its laces.

Tim

I met my friend Tim for lunch near Gleason's Gym. He is as bald as a bare truth and as hairless as a Chihuahua.

When I met him a couple of years ago I knew he would become one of my best friends. My wife and I went out with his wife and him for dinner. She is not bald. We had fun in the sun even though there was no sun in New York at night.

I liked that he was English. They speak better than we do. And they don't look for simple solutions like the liberals who think that guns rather than people shot the seventeen children in Parkland, Florida.

Did I tell you that he is bald? I think that is what I like the most about him. Except maybe the accent.

I tell him that America never should have revolted against England. I'd rather be English than American. They have so much manners and class.

Tim is seventeen years younger than me. I could be his father. Yet he ain't heavy and he looks like my brother. I don't know if Tim was alive when the Righteous Brothers were singing.

Whatever. He is a friend of my friendship in an English garden. He's a long and winding road.

We are trim buddies. It's nice. I don't know why. I don't know why he is bald but I like it.

LIFE AS IT IS

Taxed

I m not sure of taxes. I got away with a million and never made them up. But death is certain. I will be paying that bill the rest of my after-life.

I am pissed at God for putting me on this earth and planning to take me off. He will throw me into outer space like a javelin.

Anyhow why should I pay my taxes when my senators waste my money on fancy meals, clothes, mansions and prostitutes?

I never stole from one of my clients. I only stole from a corrupt government who stole from me while it wolfed down frogs' legs.

When I die will my wife lay me out on Limoges dishes and drink my blood from thousand dollar cups?

I don't care if she takes me out of the cupboard and lays me bare on our thirty-thousand-dollar antique table. My dead face will be as beautiful as porcelain.

Morning Lottery Ticket

I am up all night. I don't sleep well anymore now that I am coming closer to death and am worried that I will fall into a pail of bones.

I go to bed at 2 A.M. after watching a comedy—"The Death of Stalin." I don't crack a smile. It stinks.

I wake up thirty times during the night and finally get out of bed at ten thirty after resetting the alarm five times.

I go down for coffee and buy a lottery ticket. Two friends of mine have won a million dollars each in the lottery in the last six months.

I never bought tickets before. What the heck, if luck is in the air I might catch onto some of it.

I scratch the ticket. I don't even know how to read it. If I won I wouldn't realize it. I am beginning to misunderstand the simplest things. How can I be a winner when I don't even understand what it means to win? I cannot read my numbers.

Life is a Gift in a Tiffany Box

The world is coming back to me like a friend that I ignored. I no longer look away. Time passes and then dies and I want to revive it from its graveyard lament.

Life is such a small package. It is a gift in a Tiffany box that is glamourous for a while until it sparkles away into infinite disappearance.

So what comes and goes until it disappears into some other person's memory and goes to sleep in a sort of jest.

I am sitting in my room contemplating what I have done and if I have anything left to do on this borrowed highway.

I am jewelry. I am precious. I love myself like a vase of misplaced narcissism. You would like to wear me on your ring finger but I would rather wear you like a diamond bracelet.

I put my hands in a sink of soap bubbles and wash my fingers so that I am as clean as freshly wiped dishes.

Time Left

So I probably have about twenty years left. What have I accomplished when accomplishment is a middle class word for reverse failure?

Have I lived a good life? How the hell should I know? Do I want to know? I dare to not care.

Was I good to a woman? Forty-five years married to the same woman shows that I am more than show and less than doing what I must.

I brought up a son. I'm not sure he loves me. When I went to jail and he was fourteen, I think he lost trust in me as if my going off was my decision and not some stupid judge's.

Well it has all been a pretty good show. Like I was in the audience at a theatre watching the Rockettes dance.

I am closing in on the big round up. I'll wrestle a bull or two and get thrown over a fence where I break my neck and die in rodeo glory.

Your View of Me

My life is whatever it is with all the details sewn into the sleeves so that I can't shake them loose. I am the recalcitrance that becomes bold on cocaine or champagne.

Days pass like soap slipping out of my hands and I jump into the bath water to drown before I get caught in the drain.

Love is something I can't do without and can't understand when knowledge steps three steps to the left and tries to convince me that it is other than it is.

How many days do I have left before I disappear into a fairy tale of death and find solace in unconscious loneliness riding bronco clouds at a radio of desperation?

Tomorrow represents some version of the past and the past predicts what will become of me when I start unbecoming in enchanted woods.

If I could spend all my days with you I would because I only know myself in looking at your view of me and realizing that I might really be loveable.

My Insanity

If I were real would you be false and what difference would it make if you didn't know me for the person I wasn't when the rain curtains came down on my living room windows?

I entered your disappearing house and found coziness in your antique furniture and your beautiful hovering around me like a butterfly in a coat of many colors. Joseph's sister with wings.

Love is the failure to achieve hate and hate is closing your eyes rather than to accept death in smoked salmon lying on a bed of cream cheese on a bagel..

My brain is fractured not from a fall on a skateboard but from a hammer breaking confusion into the cinder blocks of my ideological insistences.

Sometimes things that don't make sense make sense and intelligence becomes an afterthought that can't find its starting gate in a disappearing race course.

Nice of you to visit my insanity which must be a frightening window in a broken room where the I-phone is your only way to reach me.

My Apothecary

I am in and out of the temporal like a wish bone looking for its wish. It doesn't matter that I find myself inconvenient because nothing is easily true.

I love you. No I don't. But I love you, Lauren, my apothecary who mixes pharmaceuticals for my pleasure. I am the measure of your affection.

I know you better than myself because I don't know myself at all. I am disappearance in a nutshell.

We've crossed many a mile without feet as we danced on our torsos like cartoons. We get along when we are not getting along the road.

As I get closer to you I get farther from myself and find that I am different from who I was now that I am becoming the future's beacon.

My Wife

I Don't Really Please You

I come home early from the gym and surprise my wife. She is pleased. I am pleased. As the Beatles sang, "Please, please me oh yeah, like I please you."

But most of the time I don't really please you. And you do please me. So what do I have to do with this song?

I don't know. I like the music. I like the possible love in the rain falling in our hearts.

I suppose it's, "hard to reason with you."

It's not so easy to reason with me. Well, a little easier ever since I started taking my daily Lithium.

We have pleased each other for forty-five years. I suppose that deserves a song. I would have sung it to you when I walked in the door but I don't sing too well. In fact, I am at a distance from the key.

You are the song that comes in and out of my life. Like playing an old Beatle's record that I have listened to many times before.

Tea Sandwiches at the St. Regis

I went back to the St. Regis tea room with my wife. I have been dating the same woman for over forty years. Repetition is a compliment and continuity is a place to keep going.

I like walking down Madison Avenue with her. Particularly on a Sunday when it is not that busy. I picture us in the store windows as fashionable dummies.

If I didn't love her I wouldn't have found myself in her consistency. In my early teens I wanted to jump from one woman to another. Now I just want to jump on Lauren like a stationary bike.

The maître d shows us to a booth in the corner. The harp music wraps around us like a horse hair cover on a horse drawn carriage in St. Moritz.

Lauren orders smoked salmon and capers. I have my usual tea sandwiches. She has green tea. I have Darjeeling.

Love is a surprise that keeps confronting you. It's as neat and happy as tea sandwiches. It is proper. I eat the air around your pretty face.

I have been at the St. Regis Hotel a hundred times. I have been with Lauren thousands. I like multiplication. It makes me feel secure.

I live in an era of divorce. That's not my game. I will walk down Madison Avenue with Lauren until I die.

Rendezvous in the Park

I have valued the value of disappearing values and have run after the sun to brighten up my face in a mirror.

I come and go and go again. I am motion in a blender and a glass of juice. I spill the pits on my lap.

You don't know me. Well, I don't even know me. I am different and strange and on the edge of the ledge.

Do you want to get together in the park after midnight and pick blades of grass while we share a box of crackerjacks?

I have spent decades with you but I still have a fair amount of dollars in my wallet with your surprise face on my bill.

Relationship holds the surprise of consistency and I don't know where you came from but you are still there after all the hub bub.

My Downfall

I used to be rich; now I have the pass-me-down trappings. I live in my old apartment because my wife owns it.

When I lost my money and went to jail I thought of the stock brokers in the Depression jumping from their windows.

Why would I commit suicide when my failure set me free? I no longer have to dress up in a suit every day and go to an office. I want to be irresponsible of responsibility.

Everybody in jail knew me as a pro boxer and as a rapper—"The Renegade Jew." That's pretty cool for a forty-six year old, Jewish poet, insurance salesman.

A group of blacks came over to me when I arrived and said, "The Renegade Jew's in the house."

Back on the street I was a failed businessman. In jail I was the man. I was cool. I was looked up to like a guy who beat the system. It was like a long termer instead of a nerd doing a meagre two years.

I got out of jail in 1995. I am still living like I did before jail without the vacations, without the money, without the stupidity of selling insurance to burning houses like Obama sold medical insurance to preconditions or people who already had cancer or heart attacks.

Blue Guitar

I really don't care about you whoever you are. Because I don't know you. I play you on the blue guitar.

But you are not changed. Because whatever the color of the guitar the tune remains the same.

I sing myself. That is all I know and all I need to know. I am what I am and as distinct as ham from a Muslim and a Jew.

Keats said , "'Beauty is truth, truth beauty." I don't think so. Everything is truth. Except a lie which is a lying truth.

You do not play the blue guitar. I do. I am everything. I am the guitar, the music and the blue.

I play things exactly as they are. I have no idea what that is. I play me as who I am whoever I be. I am me. Whoopee. I hope I last awhile longer.

Marjorie Stoneman High School

So many of my poems having so little to do with my life and lost in their language like Hansel and Gretel amongst the trees, in the woods, in the tales of fairies.

I want to come back to the real and reel it in like bass in a lake in the Adirondacks when I was twelve, a guest of my best friend's, Barneys, family.

I want to return to the first time I kissed Lauren on the lips on Freedom Road in my dad's borrowed Buick Riviera.

I want to go back to 1989 when I won the A-competition singles at North Shore Tennis Club in Bayside.

I want to win first place again at the New Jersey Ski Racing Association in slalom. The course was solid ice. I was one of the few that didn't crash.

I want to knock out another pro at Trump Plaza in Atlantic City.

I want to pick up my Ph.D. in literature again at CUNY.

I want to leave insanity, confusion and vagueness on my doorstep and pull up my bipolar door mat and put it inside my coop.

I want to greet the FBI as they raid my office at 120 Wall Street. They didn't know that I had already been arrested by their Delaware office.

The feds make a lot of mistakes. Like failing to confront Nikolas Cruz at Marjory Stoneman High School. Like allowing him to kill seventeen people. The cops were stuck in their own dreams. They were their own screams that never happened.

Conquering Jail

When I went to jail every other word was "Mother fucker." It made me ill. I always loved my mother and although she was gorgeous I never wanted to fuck her.

I was sent to the black dormitory. The CO's thought I would be scared. But I boxed, rapped and hung out with blacks.

And when I walked over to the blacks they said to me, "Yo, the Renegade Jew is in the house." My first album was "The Renegade Jew." My name was AD and it was advertised in "Source Magazine." I was a star in jail. A forty-six year old Jewish star.

Some of the other guys saw me knock a guy out on the "Sean O'Grady's Thursday Night Fights" on national television. All the cons watched the fights in the rec room.

Who was I? I didn't know myself. I was a cool "mother fucken" middle aged guy. Back in the insurance business I was a crook but in jail I was a star.

So when you tell me you are afraid of jail I say, "Fuck you." It was the best two years I spent of my life.

Somehow I fit in. Jail couldn't beat me. I beat it. I think I could even handle the death penalty unlike the crybabies on death row.

I am what I am. Better than jail or punishments. I celebrate myself unlike Whitman's song of himself, but like a real man not a gay nurse.

I Am Madison Avenue

I still live on Madison Avenue. That's pretty grand. I sweep the rich atmosphere up in my hand. I shoot it out like a marble and pick it up like it's time to go home.

This is a rich avenue. When I moved here I had some money and some pretense to class. Now I am a boxing trainer who is sort of trash. My life went down when my money crashed. I am what is left of the last.

By a miracle I still live here among the elderly rich and the trust fund babies. I am spoiled jam on a hot piece of bread. I am alive and I am dead. Is that a cockroach under the table or death's beetle.

Seventy years old is embarrassing. But I can still do one hundred push-ups and what the heck—I am far from dead.

Maybe I more than live on Madison Avenue. Maybe I am Madison Avenue. The limousines ride across my back and put street signs behind my ears.

So many rich shops at my elbows. I am a wardrobe of wishes and a hopeful basket of designer clothes. I am tailored. I fit wherever I am.

Tripping

My wife calls me and I tell her about my tripping over my own feet. She is so sympathetic and treats me like a boo boo on a banana.

Her voice is sweet. I cover myself in her sugar and purse my lips to kiss her over the phone.

She is who she is and when she is not I appreciate her like a multimillion dollar painting.

I am glad to gather her sympathy up into a bowl like a human treat in a delicious sunrise.

She loves me. She loves me a lot. Not not. And there is something grand about the piano keys of her melodic whispers.

She is what I bought into forty-five years ago and I feel that my investment has risen from the edgy to the beveled shapes of affection.

WHO I AM

Hello

I am a person who isn't a person who is someone else's vision of life in its preexistence.

I say hello to myself and don't answer because I do not know my other self who is opening up a conversation with me.

If I knew me better I would get along better with my shadow falling from my shoulders and my shadow rising to meet me.

I am the answer to your questions and the question about your answers which I don't understand.

You are me and I am you and the two will do to create a gathering crowd in a boisterous field.

It's been nice being me but there is something unreal about it and I find it is hard to recognize myself blowing bubbles under the lake.

Me

If you were me you would see why I prefer the company of myself to the elbow rubs of strangers.

I get to know me in the dark streets and I find myself alone in the introspection of my room.

I shy away from others because I am shy and because I can only get to know myself when I am alone.

The rest of the world doesn't exist for me because I find variety in my solicitude and my removal from the storm.

I received my education by turning away from the plentitude of grass on my front lawn.

I decided to share my life with my wife and held onto her hand like an inclusion. We are part of the same body on a continual walk down the aisle.

Doggie

I am beginning to lose my mind. I can't find it. It finds me and tells me that I am gone. "Oh where, oh where/ Has my little dog gone?"

My brain barks. It is not a tree. It is a dog that leashes out to me and shits on my shoes.

I have no control over my thoughts. All I can do is chose to take them lightly. To not care. To strip my soul bare and dare to ignore the outside world.

I am a fractured brain. I am broken pottery. I am pieces of myself on the floor under the dining room table.

Sometimes I can ride on a raft of thought. Others I drown in a river of no return. Death is no return. I can't bring it to the supermarket like bottles to get five cents back.

I take myself out for a walk. I am an English bulldog. I am so ugly that I find myself cute. I am in love with myself. It doesn't matter to me if I am alone in this emotion.

It is in being singularly self-loving that importance is raised like a patriotic flag. I am a country. I am a dog. I am my own best friend.

Alive

I was alive. Now I am dead. I miss being alive. It was a very conscious trip where I was aware that I was aware as I drank down the air like ginger ale.

God likes me because I am not afraid to disagree with him. He does not like little pussies running around him like cats.

I am a man. God created a man. He is not gender neutral. He hates men who are women and women who are men. He created both to be either and not to be the same and not to have sex with the same sex without procreation.

I got a lot of balls. It's not only the physical kind. It's the spiritual brazenness to go against the odds when the odds are against you.

I do not know why little girls want to be men and little men want to be girls. You can't be what you're not and you're not a lot when you cut off your organs.

It's not that transgenders are sick but you sure can't say such confusion is well. If you can't be what you be you are the magnificent degradation of a lie.

The Stranger

You call me an original hippy or a modernist. I don't know what labels mean. I think they are used to paste on jars of Schmucker's.

You say that Meursault got angry in *The Stranger* and killed the Arab. You miss the point. He felt numb. It was an act of wild-eyed indifference.

And when he was executed he felt bland in comparison to the hate that was raining down on his execution parade.

I am missing the world. Not missing it but removed from it. I am separation's isolation in a lamb's sweater of warmth.

You don't know me. Either do I. I don't want to be introduced to me. I am what I am without the intrusion of definitions.

If you shake my hand it will fall off. I am isolated from myself. I am the contusions after a fall down the stairs.

I am the promise of your redemption.

Solid as a Rock

I don't know if I exist or I am just someone others thoughts. Maybe I am the being of his mind or the reference to another person.

Look at me and do you see a version of you somewhere behind your retinue where insight starts.

I am as solid as a rock and as soft as an emotional woman. I don't know who I am because I am possibly not.

When I will be gone I will be gone and all these splendiferous thoughts in my head will dribble down to puddle with the average person's thoughts.

Will there be any pieces of me left in the disappearing cloud where rain is always about to fall and never lands on our galoshes?

Now I see me now I don't. I don't really care. When you're playing a losing game you just have to get used to losing. God is the house. He is a mean casino.

Central Park Blow Up

I have found the intelligence of a computer in the framework of my wizard bones. I am more than that. I am this and that and the intuition of a pear on a tree.

I will see me when I see. I will take off my blinders and follow my intuition into a jar of cinnamon. I wake up in the morning confused and not knowing whether I am who I seem or a failed dream.

To know myself is to not know you. I forget who you are and lose myself in an alley in a failing city on the west side of everything that is central.

There is a monument to me between my ears. It is a statue on marble of me being the last man on earth in a failed sunset in the licked shadows of yellow.

I find myself in Central Park. I am blown up by a terrorist who puts dynamite in a bag and shares the explosion with me as I drop down from a tree.

The Illusion of Meaning

The day goes as it goes without much consequence in a kind of indifference where the moon is hidden behind a living room shade.

There is not much meaning when meaning is an illusion tied to a balloon and flying up into the disappearing black sky.

I do not even know if anyone notices that I am here on this planet floating an exciting brain in a drainpipe of no expectations.

I am here. I appear. And then I bumble into my indifference like a zombie who is not really dead but shuffles like a corpse.

I guess I am what you are not and in the confusion I am a forget-me-not, an indelible impression.

I am nothing but I am it all and I will arrive at death with a water bucket so that I can sprinkle the garden with who I am and who I am not.

One Regret

I have done a lot of things in my life. I am a swimming pool which I dove into and swam around like a puppy with a broken neck.

I am here. I am there. I am on the bottom of the pool. I am in a tube riding a still wave as my brother jumps into summer.

Days peel off from me like scotch tape and I am stuck to the drain pipe pulling the wetness of life out of its presentation.

I earned a Ph.D. Boy was I smart. I studied life while I ignored it and I skimmed credibility from the scum like I was trying to reproduce meaning.

When I boxed at the Mirage Hotel in Las Vegas I felt what it was like to be hit out of my stupor into the startling abuse of life.

It's been a good life. I have one regret, that God made me temporary and that when I get old enough I will drown in a glass.

I will be poured into my coffin like bottled water.

Escape from the Language

What I am doing doesn't matter because what is done is done and I am trying to figure out what is not is what it is. And it all doesn't matter but it is all part of this poem.

I am trying to escape from the language. I am trying to engage in the pragmatism of what happens when it doesn't happen and what translates from discourse to impracticality.

I am me whoever I be and in the magnificence of me I find the shelter of a storm that is hidden by blankets.

Soon I am going out to lunch with my wife. Words will evaporate and the drizzle will make me close to her wandering on Madison Avenue.

If I cough will it be a precursor of my death around the corner as I pass the street signs of seventy years old.

So don't speak to me whoever you are because I am not listening to idle chatter. I don't mean my wife. I want to hear her. She can talk my ears off and I will hold them like apricots.

Vail

I don't know whether I am all words or whether the words mean anything. I think I'd rather float above the light powder of words on the back bowls of Vail.

I don't want to mean. I want to exist. I am happening in the interstices between pointing and indication.

I have stopped reading other poets. I can't understand them. I am shoveling into my heart and lifting the soil of my love onto the fringes of the graveyard.

On my tombstone I will etch, "David was wonderful."

I know it. You don't. What do I care when I am about to meet my unmaker and find solace in the miracle of my undoing?

Words

I like words more than reality. It is not the words themselves but the integument that joins them in balls of yarn.

I never intend to mean. I am the meaning that spins out of control and defines me as me who I am or am not. I never know. I glow.

I brush my teeth with language. I am words bouncing into each other and light cavities on the edge of aching.

But this time I will write a book that transcends words and arrives in the backseat kissing my wife who was then my girlfriend when my older brother drove us home in my dad's Lincoln.

I want to dip my paragraphs in the concrete and use them as blocks to support a skyscraper of meanings.

I am going to try to be real. I will be the substance of substance and intellectual integrity of my body making sense.

I will be the rhythm that catches the music and the orchestra of being the firm meaning of my own surprise existence.

I am here. I am there. I am the accident that happens every time I try to make meaning out of the nothing that is and the something that isn't.

Obama in the Sky

I gave my book, "Obama in the Sky with Diamonds" to my friend at the gym.

It is a condemnation of Obama.

It is truth between book covers.

It is the sadness of facing the face of man's inhumanity.

It is the burning head of a progressive's hair as we are led by his stupid grin to the cave of awkward despair.

When I was young I was a communist.

Like Obama.

Obama is Putin in black face.

When I realized that fascists killed less people than communists

I tied myself up with the bars of ritualistic fervor and learned respect

From the trains running on time and life as something with levers and restrictions.

Obsessed

So you see that I don't see because I am lost in the circus of myself even after Barnum and Baily has closed down.

It is not that I am obsessed with myself. It is only that I don't know anyone else and I feel a close rapport with my thoughts.

It's not that I ignore you but that you don't really exist and I don't want to waste my time dancing in the dark with the dark.

Better to dress up like a blanket and crawl inside myself like rumpled sheets hiding from the air-conditioning.

God sent me through this world like a wandering donut, snacking on myself, pulling pieces from my frosting.

I would shake your hand but you don't have a hand and stumps creep me out even though that's not a nice thought to coddle.

I am me and me is I and identification is a byproduct of loneliness as I walk the back trails inside my mountain.

Writing

I feel like writing today. I don't feel like writing to day. I am written by my thoughts and my jumbled language.

I am a poet.

Big deal. I am the words that find their ways into sentences and startle me into thoughts that I have never thought before in the junkyard among scraps.

I've got to do something with my time. Something meaningful. I've got to recreate the world in a pail of sand.

I have to build a sandcastle and put down a deposit on my rent.

When the waves fall over me I fall over and learn that confusion is not an escape from reality but a new form of confrontation with my hidden self.

So I guess I am writing even though I'm not sure of what I am doing. I'd like to write ten books, put them in my book bag and hang out in front of my old high school where I did so badly and no one ever thought that I would become a walking library.

Doggie

I am beginning to lose my mind. I can't find it. It finds me and tells me that I am gone. "Oh where, oh where/ Has my little dog gone?"

My brain barks. It is not a tree. It is a dog that leashes out to me and shits on my shoes.

I have no control over my thoughts. All I can do is chose to take them lightly. To not care. To strip my soul bare and dare to ignore the outside world.

I am a fractured brain. I am broken pottery. I am pieces of myself on the floor under the dining room table.

Sometimes I can ride on a raft of thought. Others I drown in a river of no return. Death is no return. I can't bring it to the supermarket like bottles to get five cents back.

I take myself out for a walk. I am an English bulldog. I am so ugly that I find myself cute. I am in love with myself. It doesn't matter to me if I am alone in this emotion.

It is in being singularly self-loving that importance is raised like a patriotic flag. I am a country. I am a dog. I am my own best friend.

Computer

The other day I got lost in the rain forest of my computer and found naked pygmies dancing around me.

I had forgotten how to access my access and couldn't find the map of my icons in the blue screen of my invention.

I spent three hours playing with the missing logic of the technical world until I realized that I was not on my computer at home and the one in the gym had to icons

I was lost in the world of modern keys and I couldn't find thought patterns in my Tabula Raza.

I became worried that I had lost my mind again and that the nothing that made sense didn't really have a magnetic rationale.

I called my neurologist and made an appointment. I am losing what I have lost but am realizing the confusion of my conclusion.

I am seventy years old and waiting to die in a jumble of wires. I don't care. I am stupidly brave.

Gleason's Boxing Gym

Breakfast

I don't have to be at Gleason's Gym until about three o'clock P.M. It is nine o'clock A.M. I don't have as many students as I did back in the day. What day? What job?

I teach boxing. I'm the only Ph.D. who was a former CEO who is a boxing coach. I don't know why I am doing this work. It just happened. I became what I wasn't and shook the fun from me like a dog frisking water off his fur.

I go downstairs and buy coffee, a chocolate donut and a green Gatorade. The joys of breakfast. I want to eat my thumbnails. I want to lick my nose. I want to wake my wife and kiss her neck.

Life is a multitude of little things. I am playing with my thoughts like Lego blocks. It's the little things that don't count. I count. I measure the world on my fingers.

The day is turning out like any other day. Except it is different in that that I have an overview. I see the whole scheme of who is me.

I be as a solid presence. I am totally total. I am the day that got away and returned as a memory of what it was. I am in touch with my touch and elicit a world of fantasy which is real.

Joining Gleason's

I walked into Gleason's Boxing Gym near Madison Square Garden in 1984. Back in the day there were no white boys and no girls except Martha Graham.

It looked kind of slummy and I didn't visualize spending the rest of my life there where I didn't care about punishment and greeted broken noses with "how do you do" I am a friend of you.

As I sunk into the environment I left the Upper East Side world behind and became a low-class version of my past cool.

Each morning I looked forward to my beatings and felt body punches like hugs, broken ribs like sex.

Sometimes I can't tell the difference between hurt and hurting, love and punishment.

I am not a masochist. I am just a poor excuse for pain and an equestrian riding towards his death on saddle soap.

Sparring with Phil

I spar six rounds with Phil. He has been my student for twenty years. I haven't taught him a thing in ten years. He has already learned what I had to say.

Yet he keeps coming back like a faithful friend, a pup, a best acquaintance.

He has been lifting a lot of weights. He has bulked up. He is balanced like a thick chair on a porch.

He gets the better of me. It's frustrating to lose to your student. It is a sad confrontation with one's diminishing.

I am disappearing while Phil is pummeling me. I am the absence of yesterday's presence. I am the smoke that rises from a cigar.

I am worried about losing my foothold in the world. He has the solidity of footwork on a cliff. He won't fall. I will end up on the ground.

Will I look up at the medics? Or will I look down at my bewildered reflection in a pool of sweat?

I Feel Like a Movie Star

Some guy at Gleason's Gym comes over to me and says, "I looked you up on Google. You're cool. You fought Hector Camacho at the Taj Mahal in Atlantic City."

I did. But it wasn't a fight. It was an exhibition. They tell me I looked pretty good. Who is they? I don't remember.

When you get hit in the head a lot you begin to lose it. You find your head under the living room couch looking for a familial home and a discarded ashtray to hide your remains in.

I like it when people recognize me and I don't know who they are. I feel like a movie star although I'm far too intelligent to be part of the celluloid tribe. I am more intellectual than my diction or my speeches.

I'm constantly getting bumped into and caught in a passerby's blink. I am eye goo. I am candy. I am who you think I am when I am probably not.

I am a rumor about nothing that spreads around like it is important. I am a conversation spread out on a Flora Danica plate at a rich dinner party.

Ryan

I am at the front desk in Gleason's Gym bullshitting with Ryan. He is the gatekeeper. You have to pass by him to get in. He's a younger version of me. I am he. We are we.

A Columbian girl comes in and we all start talking. She asks if there are any weights. I take her to the back of the gym and show them to her. I take her to my office and show her my pictures in magazines and my trophies.

I want to convince her to become my student. You never can tell. I give her my coaching card so that she can call me.

I take her back to the front desk and wave goodbye to her. Ryan says that Don, who also works the desk, asked why Ryan let me show the girl around. Don's my age. We tend to get nosey. Who cares? Caring is an obsession for the young. It's for people who have nothing at stake.

Lady, that was her name. Lady. Can you be a Lady and a female boxer? Is the contradiction like punching yourself in the face?

I don't know if Lady will sign up with me? Things get slow when you're a seventy year old trainer. I am slow. I know and I forget to know. She is the Lady and the Tramp.

At First

I'm not sure that I work in a gym. Have I become that lowly? When I first was chauffeured up to Gleason's Boxing Gym I was a millionaire.

A minor millionaire. One who could do anything whenever he wanted with whatever money he didn't care.

And now I am working as a boxing coach for nickels and dimes. My life has become small change and I have little to say about myself.

I have sacrificed lifestyle for small potatoes. I feel like I'm in a field in Iowa. I am laid out in a ditch. Maybe I'm corn.

Not that it matters. I am happy in my ways. I am way to the side of awesome responsibility.

I can't really call this job work. It is a way of passing the day in my sidestepping loneliness and not having to muscle with a business career.

I Am Not a Star

I am at Gleason's Gym hardly teaching anyone. Oh where oh where have my students gone? Oh where Oh where have they gone?

I'm sitting in my office jerking off. Not really. I look at my walls and see my picture in *People Mag., New York Mag. Time Out Mag. and Men's Journal Mag.*

I am a star. Not me. I am the reflection of my radiance in the accidental juxtaposition with the media.

I have been running through my money. My money has been running through me. I am losing my hope and I am hoping I can find some hope in what is vanishing.

My substitute career as a trainer is beginning to disappear. I don't know how much longer I can tell myself that I am doing OK when I am not.

It doesn't matter much. I am seventy. I will be dead before I turn around and whistle Dixie three times.

I am preparing for my end. My end is preparing for me. The end.

At The Door

Two doormen are downstairs at my building. I forget their names.
I have known them twenty years. I have gotten hit a lot in the head.
Professional boxing is not good for a clear mind if you were once a
college professor.

They call me Rocky. I like that. I tell them Sylvester Stallone was
a fraud and never had a real fight.

The Puerto Rican nameless doorman tells me that Robert De Nero
was a real fighter. I tell him that he was a pussy, never had a fight and
didn't even graduate from college.

"De Nero couldn't last in the ring with me for twenty seconds and
he has the nerve to challenge our President who at least played high
school football."

I'm sick of all these pretend boxers. William Defoe, John Leguizamo
(a nice guy) all trained at Gleason's Gym. Even Hillary Swank. At
least they all showed up. Where was De Nero hiding?

Usher was there too. He didn't look bad. Shia Le Bouef was
hitting the bags. I didn't notice because I didn't like his persona and his
persona was indicative of his lack of depth.

James Franco was there a few times. I didn't think that he would
hit on women. Did he? What do I know?

The Puerto Rican doorman checks out what I'm saying about De
Nero on his I-phone. True is true. I am true blue. I am the color of the
sky. I am losing my mind among the clouds.

Were those ten thousand sparring sessions, nine amateur fights, six
pro fights, and sixty white collar fights worth the confusion I am feeling
when I try to remember the forgotten days?

Florida

It doesn't matter as long as I stabilize on the end of a rational pill. As long as I can figure out which foot goes first when I stroll along Madison Avenue with my wife and she complains that I am not paying attention to whatever she is saying to me. I try. I am as vague as the gray sky.

Florida

Nicholas Cruz was having a good time shooting up his ex-classmates. The liberals blame it on the guns. The conservatives blame it on mental illness.

Seventeen dead. Seventeen wed with death at an adolescent age. And we wonder who is at fault. I don't. It is the essence of America. We have become a creepy country that swarms around the gunpowder landscape like worms.

Americans deal out death like dice from a gamblers cup.

They call Nikolas Cruz a suspect. He is no suspect. He is the killer. It's as obvious as the apologies on a confused killer's face.

Cruz had become expelled from his school for being so recalcitrant that he couldn't blend with the other idiots. Imagine flunking out of a dumb high school. Cruz had a low emotional IQ.

He didn't have enough discipline to be disciplined. He is the confusion of gophers ducking from his own rifle on an open field.

Mark

Mark comes down to Gleason's Gym for his first lesson in two weeks. He has been sick. The flu will do if I can't think of a better box of tissues. He is planning on making a movie about me.

We fight three round and we beat the shit out of each other. I am his coach and shouldn't hit him so hard. My old coach, Hector, is standing ringside and I always show off for him.

Mark usually fights eight rounds. Today he stops at three. He has been fighting the flu and now he is fighting me.

I'm not sure I should have hit him so hard. After all, he is writing a movie about my boxing career. That's pretty something, something.

But then again I would not want to disrespect him by babying him. He can take a punch and he knows how to put one on a platter like a pheasant.

Marc is fifty-seven and I am seventy. Age is indicative of nothing if you are not sick. We fight like two vindictive old codgers.

I wonder if the movie will be made. I see celluloid in the sky and watch my future high above me. My life could change. Or it might remain the same. Or it might get worse. Will I get knocked out like in Denver?

Going to Work

I set my alarm for eight and got up at six. I watched Channel One and got ready to go to the gym where I teach. Gleason's is a legend. I am someone who wandered in there thirty years ago.

What did Channel One say? The F train isn't running.

I come and I go but what do I really know? I am wading into a giant wave in the Atlantic. I am drowning before the water breaks over my head.

I get on the Five train which is running on the Six track. It runs local, then express. It drops me at Fulton Street where I catch the A train to High Street in Dumbo.

When the train goes slow I want to beat my head against the door. I want to shout. I want to let it all in and out.

In twenty years I'll be ninety. That's old to be alive and old to be dead. I am passing through my life like a train passing through its stations.

I arrive at Gleason's Boxing Gym. Perhaps someone will beat my head in. I don't need the train. I can die at a sport. I will swallow a boxing glove. I will hang myself from the laces.

Death in the Kennels

I have died and gone to doggie heaven amongst the poodles and the gray haired schnauzers.

Not really. But heck I am seventy and expect to soon hear the barking of death in the kennels.

I don't care. I don't know where I will be going or where I won't wander into the ashes of my cremation.

I shouldn't be boxing anymore but what's the difference when difference no longer makes a difference and death is a blank slate?

I come and go and go on the underside of a marked deck of cards as I win what I don't deserve to win and pull a tuna out of the sea for good luck.

I have suddenly gone fishing. I will die at the bottom of the sea with all my forget-me-nots which I have forgot.

Careers

I am leaving Gleason's Gym at eleven o'clock A.M. I don't have any more students so there is no sense in sticking around like a bored fly on orange sticky paper.

It feels like this is another career coming to a close. I am reaching the end of the end and the future beginnings will be few and far between.

I have run out of occupations. I have been a college teacher, an insurance mogul and a pro fighter turned coach.

I suppose I could go back to a university and try to dig up a job as a poetry teacher. I've published five books and a thousand poems.

But I am no one. I am unrecognized. I am a cat who has stepped aside to let pussies moan and take over the field. Poets are not men. They are hysterical words.

I am not famous. I am simply the genius who was ignored by those who resented my diversity in a land divided into different agricultural products.

I arrive home and write this poem. It's an effort. It's an attempt. I don't even care if it is good or bad as long as it surprises me.

About Lunch

It's time for lunch. Lunch has invited me to its celebration. I walk past E.A.T. but don't stop in. Their sandwiches are a little small and never fill me up.

How so? I am only one hundred and fifty pounds.

Anyhow I go to Marche Madison another block uptown. I get a bagel with smoked salmon and cream cheese. I buy a container of orange juice.

I go home. I kiss my wife hello. Not really. She doesn't like the way I shave and doesn't want to offer up her cheek to my slaughter.

I ask her if I can eat in the dining room with her or does she want me to go back to my room. Back to the room it is. She is almost as tired of me as I am. She is diddling on her I-phone and doesn't want to be disturbed.

I turn on Fox news. I watch for ten minutes while I eat my bagel. I don't know what I watch because my memory is something that has sewn itself up in yesterday's pocket.

I am sitting at my desk writing poetry. Fighting and writing are my things. I said that to the warden at Schuylkill Federal Prison Camp. He ignored me. I don't need a memory to write. Every word is a new invention. It comes clear out of the future like a king's carriage galloping backwards.

I Don't Care

I am beginning to know myself. Not really. I don't have a clue. I just deeply dig into the denseness of whoever I am.

What do I care if I am this or that? I am nothing if not anything and something that eludes me like snowstorms in Florida.

What I feel is hard to determine because it is nothing in a circular pattern of thoughts.

It's not in the knowing myself but in the hugging my AstroTurf that I come close to being tackled in a football game.

There is nothing as warm as the feeling of getting knocked out in a pro fight. You get lost in your unconsciousness.

Life becomes illustrious and I am a Renaissance painting in the Metropolitan Museum of personality.

The less I know about me the deeper I explore the variables that make me stand up and salute the flag of myself.

At Gleason's

I fought three rounds with a thirty-five year old Korean student today. He got tired so we quit.

I am a miracle. I am seventy years old and I can go all day, hey, hey, hey, I'm something else and other than normal.

My son is married to a Korean woman. They don't have a child yet. I'm in no rush. I already had my child.

After my Korean student I boxed three rounds with Mongo. Mongo is two hundred and seventy pounds and was an ex-football player.

I practiced hitting Mongo in the head because I wanted him to work on slipping punches.

Slipping at his weight? Doubtful but he did it. He is a jolly monster. I should probably enter him in a tournament.

I fought six rounds and I am a dead man walking. I kiss my hand. I want to marry me. I love that I am defying death while I am fighting my way into heaven.

Foragers' Lunch

I had sushi from Foragers for lunch. I love it. I don't know what is in it. I don't like to define things because when you tie them down they go stale.

Actually, I had lunch at least a few hours ago. Not seeing the wrapped package I have no idea what's in it. Who cares? I dare to face the great unknown with a grin.

I know nothing. I know everything. I am wearing invisible blindfolds so that you can't see me seeing what I don't see.

I am a horse in the nineteen fifties with eye patches as I pull a knife-sharpening cart down the cheap streets.

So who cares what's in the sushi? If I like it, I like it and knowing what it is will just pull my taste buds from the fish actuality to a cook book definition.

I like sushi, whatever it is. Or whatever it isn't. I skip over definitions like a frog's legs jumping from the frog.

Closeness

I woke up this morning and I was me. That's a good feeling. It's nice to be recognizable and see an etching of yourself on the wall.

I know me well. I don't know me at all. It doesn't matter when death is blowing in through the windowsill and life is something that is forgotten with last week's rain.

All I really care about is me. Narcissism is a grand display of fireworks over the Hudson during the Fourth of July.

I don't think you really exist. It's not your absence that I cherish but your brazen disappearance in the hedges.

But then again you are me and the separation is closeness. You are on the other side of me and I am the other side of you.

It doesn't matter that it matters because the long and short of it doesn't.

I Crash

So you are looking for me. Who are you? You are me on the other side of my skin. You are my internal organs made extraneous like flying cows. You are my bruised liver from a sparring session.

I fly. I am you. I fall. I am me. I am me and you as one or as two. I don't know. Do I care? No.

I am a piper cub. I crash. I am the ash after a conflagration on the ground. I am the sound of death in a disappearing wind.

You don't know me. I don't know you. It is in the interstices between knowledge that one finds the soluble and the personable.

So let me take you up to the belfry to ring the bats like bells. I will be your steeple and will weep at the joy of losing life.

I am what I am when I am what I am. It has nothing to do with ham. Imagine stupid kosher people believing that a pig is cursed. I am cursed. I regard myself like a nasty remark.

www.ingramcontent.com/pod-product-compliance
Lightning Source LLC
Chambersburg PA
CBHW051808130726
47987CB00003B/1157